SPARKPLUG

by David Judge

samuelfrench.co.uk

ISBN 978-0-573-11621-6

www.samuelfrench.co.uk
www.samuelfrench.com

For Amateur Production Enquiries

United Kingdom and World
excluding north america
plays@samuelfrench.co.uk
020 7255 4302/01

Each title is subject to availability from Samuel French, depending upon country of performance.

THINKING ABOUT PERFORMING A SHOW?

There are thousands of plays and musicals available to perform from Samuel French right now, and applying for a licence is easier and more affordable than you might think

---

From classic plays to brand new musicals, from monologues to epic dramas, there are shows for everyone.

Plays and musicals are protected by copyright law, so if you want to perform them, the first thing you'll need is a licence. This simple process helps support the playwright by ensuring they get paid for their work and means that you'll have the documents you need to stage the show in public.

Not all our shows are available to perform all the time, so it's important to check and apply for a licence before you start rehearsals or commit to doing the show.

LEARN MORE & FIND THOUSANDS OF SHOWS

Browse our full range of plays and musicals, and find out more about how to license a show

www.samuelfrench.co.uk/perform

Talk to the friendly experts in our Licensing team for advice on choosing a show and help with licensing

plays@samuelfrench.co.uk   020 7387 9373

Acting Editions

BORN TO PERFORM

Playscripts designed from the ground up to work the way you do in rehearsal, performance and study

---

Larger, clearer text for easier reading

Wider margins for notes

Performance features such as character and props lists, sound and lighting cues, and more

---

+ CHOOSE A SIZE AND STYLE TO SUIT YOU

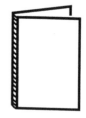

STANDARD EDITION

Our regular paperback book at our regular size

SPIRAL-BOUND EDITION

The same size as the Standard Edition, but with a sturdy, easy-to-fold, easy-to-hold spiral-bound spine

LARGE EDITION

A4 size and spiral bound, with larger text and a blank page for notes opposite every page of text – perfect for technical and directing use

---

LEARN MORE   samuelfrench.co.uk/actingeditions

MUSIC USE NOTE

Licensees are solely responsible for obtaining formal written permission from copyright owners to use copyrighted music in the performance of this play and are strongly cautioned to do so. If no such permission is obtained by the licensee, then the licensee must use only original music that the licensee owns and controls. Licensees are solely responsible and liable for all music clearances and shall indemnify the copyright owners of the play(s) and their licensing agent, Samuel French, against any costs, expenses, losses and liabilities arising from the use of music by licensees. Please contact the appropriate music licensing authority in your territory for the rights to any incidental music.

USE OF COPYRIGHT MUSIC

A licence issued by Samuel French Ltd to perform this play does not include permission to use the incidental music specified in this copy.

Where the place of performance is already licensed by the PERFORMING RIGHT SOCIETY (PRS) a return of the music used must be made to them. If the place of performance is not so licensed then application should be made to the PRS, 2 Pancras Square, London, N1C 4AG.

A separate and additional licence from PHONOGRAPHIC PERFORMANCE LTD, 1 Upper James Street, London W1F 9DE (www.ppluk.com) is needed whenever commercial recordings are used.

IMPORTANT BILLING AND CREDIT REQUIREMENTS

If you have obtained performance rights to this title, please refer to your licensing agreement for important billing and credit requirements.

The author gratefully includes the lyrics to the following compositions having received permission to reproduce these for publication.

ABOUT THE AUTHOR

David Judge is an actor, poet and playwright from Manchester. His dual heritage and working-class roots sit at the centre of his work and his visceral, vibrant, lyrical and urgent voice asks valuable questions about identity, community and loyalty in Britain today.

David trained as an actor at E15 Acting school and with the National Youth Theatre and has spent over ten years working in theatre and TV. During this time, he began writing poetry/spoken word and became a regular on the Manchester open mic scene, including a performance at the Manchester Literature Festival 2014.

His first play *Skipping Rope*, commissioned by Box of Tricks through their PlayBox playwright on attachment scheme, went on to reach the final forty of the Bruntwood Prize for Playwriting, 2015. In 2016 David was a playwright on attachment to Talawa and the Royal Exchange Theatre, Manchester.

His three plays, *Skipping Rope*, *PanLid* and *SparkPlug*, have all been finalists for the Alfred Fagon Best New Play of the Year Award.

You can follow him on Twitter @Davidsjudge

CREATIVE TEAM

DAVID JUDGE - PLAYWRIGHT

David Judge is a dual heritage poet, playwright and performer from Manchester. During his PlayBox attachment to Box of Tricks in 2014–15, David wrote his debut play *Skipping Rope* which went on to be a finalist for the prestigious Alfred Fagon Award 2015 and was shortlisted to the last 40 of the Bruntwood Prize 2015. David was Talawa writer-on-attachment with the Royal Exchange 2016–17 during which time he wrote *PanLid* (finalist for Alfred Fagon Award 2018) which was presented as part of PUSH Festival in January 2018. David was on the BBC's Hotlist 2017. He has recently completed the Channel 4 4screenwriting programme. As a spoken word artist, David regularly performs with Bad Language and has twice reached the final of spoken word competition *Word Wars*.

HANNAH TYRRELL-PINDER - DIRECTOR

Hannah trained as a director at Mountview Academy of Theatre Arts and is Joint Artistic Director of Box of Tricks. Directing credits for Box of Tricks include: *Narvik* (Liverpool Playhouse Studio 2015 and national tour 2017); *In Doggerland* (national tour); *Word:Play/NWxSW* (Regional Tour); *Picture a City* (Everyword 2012, Liverpool Playhouse); *London Tales* (Waterloo East and Nu:Write Festival, Zagreb); *Head/Heart* (national tour); *Word:Play 4* (Arcola); *True Love Waits* (Latitude, Pulse, Nu:Write Festivals); *Word:Play 3* (Theatre 503); *Whispering Happiness* (Tristan Bates); *Captain of the School Football Team* (Hotbed and Latitude festivals '09); *Word:Play 2* (Theatre 503); *Word:Play* (Union Theatre); *A Hole in the Fence* and *Rural* (White Bear). Other directing includes: *Uprising* (Monkeywood at The Lowry), *JB Shorts 11* (Joshua Brooks), *Narvik* (Everyword 2013), *100 Seel St* (The Alligator Club, Liverpool), *JB Shorts 7* (Joshua Brooks). She is a script reader for The Royal Exchange, and the Bruntwood Playwriting Prize.

KATIE SCOTT - DESIGNER

Katie is an Associate Artist of Box of Tricks and is an award-winning theatre designer based in the North-West. Upon graduating from LIPA, she was the inaugural winner of the Liverpool Playhouse Studio Prize For Theatre Design. She has since worked extensively designing for various forms of theatre and was shortlisted to be a member of the Old Vic 12 in 2017. Katie's credits include: *Peter Pan* (The Dukes, Lancaster); *Searching for the Heart of Leeds* (West Yorkshire Playhouse); *Blackout* (The Dukes, Lancaster); *Narvik* (Box of Tricks – national studio tour); *Plastic Figurines* (National Studio Tour 2015 and New Diorama 2016); *Chip Shop Chips* (Box of Tricks – national tour 2016 and 2018); *Under The Market Roof* (Junction 8); *Held* (Liverpool Playhouse Studio – winner of Liverpool Daily Post Arts Award for Best Design 2012); *We Are The Multitude* (24:7 Festival – MTA nominee Best Fringe Show); *Gargantua* (NT Connections – Lowry Young Company); *The Ballad of Rudy* (Goblin Theatre – Royal Exchange Studio); *Bluestockings* (ALRA North); *The Grid* (Young Everyman Playhouse Company – Liverpool Everyman); *Clybourne Park* (Said & Done Theatre Company – Unity Theatre Liverpool).

RICHARD OWEN - LIGHTING DESIGNER

Richard is an Associate Artist of Box of Tricks. For Royal Exchange Theatre: *Hunger For Trade, The Gatekeeper, Winterlong, Zack, Powder Monkey, Salt, The Palace of The End* (Galway Festival and Traverse Theatre, Edinburgh), *Dr Korzack's Example, Jonah and Otto, The Flags, Monster, Mojo Mickeybo, The Flags* (studio), *Christmas Is Miles Away, Come Blow Your Horn, Mayhem, Dogboy, The Rise And Fall Of Little Voice, The Happiest Days Of Your Life, Rafts And Dreams, Across Oka, Moonshed, Dead Wait, On My Birthday* and *Quids and Dimps*. Lighting designs for other companies include, *Narvik, Plastic Figurines* (Box of Tricks); *Tree* (Old Vic Theatre); *Flesh* (Monkeywood Theatre Company); *Manpower* (2DestinationLanguage); *Brassed Off, Bouncers, Educating Rita, Bedevilled* and *The Little Mermaid* (Sheffield Crucible); *The Buddy Bolden Experience* (Fittings Multimedia Arts) and

Flesh N Steel The Last Freakshow and *Edmund The Learned Pig* (Fittings Multimedia Arts in association with the Royal Exchange Theatre); *Weeding Cane* (for Weeding Cane in association with the Royal Exchange Theatre); *In The Shadow Of Trees* and *Veil* (for Horse and Bamboo Theatre Company) and *Delphic* in concert for MIF13.

CHRIS JAMES - SOUND DESIGNER

Chris is an Associate Artist of Box of Tricks and has worked with the company for more than ten years. Box of Tricks sound designs include: *Chip Shop Chips, Plastic Figurines, In Doggerland, My Arms, Whispering Happiness, Word:Play* and *Word:Play 2, A Hole In The Fence, Rural,* and *Beyond Omarska*. Other work: Associate sound designer for *Democracy* (Old Vic Theatre*); School for Scandal* (Bath Theatre Royal); *The Bargain* (National Tour); Head of Sound for *Million Dollar Quartet* (National Tour); *King and I* (National Tour; *Blood Brothers* (National Tour) and *Cabaret* (National Tour). He was a Sound and Broadcast Supervisor at Royal Opera House Muscat, in Oman from 2012 to 2017. Chris is currently Head of Sound for the UK tour of *Rock of Ages*.

HANNAH CALASCIONE - ASSISTANT DIRECTOR

Hannah is currently completing her director training at Birkbeck College on a secondment with HOME Theatre, Manchester. She completed her social sciences BA at The University of Cambridge in 2016 and then worked at Potboiler Productions first as Director/Producer's Assistant and then as Literary Development Assistant. Assisting credits include *The Little Stranger* (Film – Potboiler/Pathe/Element) and *The Maids* (HOME Theatre). Previous directing credits include *All the Little Lights* (Guildhall School of Music & Drama, CoLab); *Knots* (Theatre N16); *The Effect* (Corpus Playroom); *trade* (Corpus Playroom) and *All My Sons* (ADC Theatre). She still works as a script reader for Potboiler Productions.

MAX EMMERSON - ASSOCIATE PRODUCER

Max trained as an Arts Manager at the Liverpool Institute for Performing Arts (LIPA). He has worked as Assistant Producer for the Royal Exchange Theatre in Manchester, Bill Kenwright Productions in the West End and for Sell A Door Theatre Company in London. Since 2012, Max has been producing new writing, musicals and dance at the Edinburgh Fringe Festival and internationally. Producing credits include: *The Tempest* (Royal Exchange Theatre); The Bruntwood Prize Ceremony 2017, *The People Are Singing* (Royal Exchange Theatre); *Adam & Eve & Steve* (Kings Head Theatre, London 2017 and Edinburgh Fringe Festival 2016); *Shout! The Mod Musical* (Liverpool's Royal Court Theatre 2016 and Edinburgh Fringe Festival 2015/16); *Shake It Up Baby* (Unity Theatre, Liverpool 2016) and *Dirt, Roses, Animals & God* (Norwegian Tour 2015). Max was the first recipient of the Anthony Field Producer Prize at LIPA and successfully completed the Stage One Producers apprenticeship scheme.

BOX OF TRICKS
The new play makers

"A theatre company to watch"
THE STAGE

Box of Tricks is a Manchester-based theatre company that champions the next generation of playwrights, producing top quality new writing on local and national stages.

We are a launchpad for new talent. We commission and develop bold and original new plays from the most exciting new voices, creating ambitious and heartfelt theatre that engages, challenges and entertains. We stage new plays in Manchester and the North and tour productions to audiences nationwide.

We are the next generation. We are the new play makers.
We are Box of Tricks.

www.boxoftrickstheatre.co.uk

THANK YOU

Our playmaker Patrons: (Sue Tyrrell, John and Gloria Quayle, Kath Quick and Ed Benson); Niki Woods, Mark Fox and the University of Salford; Luke Owen; Matthew Linley; The Unity Theatre, Liverpool; Jason Done for the development of the play; our Board (Caz Brader, David Bryan, Chris Honer, Rhiannon McKay-Smith, John Quayle), Sean Croke and Marley for the promotional images, Nial Diamond and Hampton Motors.

Supported by Arts Council England, Granada Foundation.

NOTES ON STAGING

The play is set between the early 1980s and early 1990s and this should be apparent to the audience in the set, costume and sound design.

The set design can be as abstract or as naturalistic as the creative team decide. It is important that the audience knows where Dave is at any given point in the action, and also which car he is driving, however how these locations and vehicles are represented to the audience is entirely up to the creative team's discretion.

Stage directions are included as guidelines and can be interpreted freely to fit with the overall production concept.

All characters in this play are the be performed by one actor

- Indicates an interruption

... indicates a pause, waiting, searching or doing

. Is a suggestion to end the thought or breath. Please feel free to play with these to suit your performance

NOTES FOR CASTING

This play can be performed by a white male or a mix-raced male.

Please select which prologue you use depending on your casting choice.

An alternative prologue can be found on p115.

ACKNOWLEDGMENTS

Thanks to everyone included in my memory of this story.
Even the bad ones.

Also, a massive thanks to Box of Tricks for encouraging me
to tell it in this form and bringing it to life.
Thanks to all the theatres who have welcomed this story.
And the theatres who haven't...but will.

Thanks to my Great Nana and Grandad
Who taught me to believe in fairies at the end of garden.

Thanks to everyone who has interacted with me at some
point in my life.
Those moments make me, no matter how big or small.

A thanks to Jane Fallowfield and Talawa Theatre company
for their continued support and guidance.

Thank you.

X

SparkPlug received its world premiere in a production by Box of
Tricks Theatre Company, which opened at HOME, Manchester
on 14th February 2019 before embarking on a national tour.

CAST

DAVE David Judge

CREATIVE TEAM

Director	Hannah Tyrrell-Pinder
Designer	Katie Scott
Lighting Designer	Richard Owen
Sound Designer	Chris James
Assistant Director	Hannah Calascione
Associate Producer	Max Emmerson
Production Manager	Liam Whittaker
Technical Stage Manager	Adam Steed
Press & PR	Chloé Nelkin Consulting

MEMORY

This a story about me, my Dad and my family
As I remember it.
The truth of this story exists in the truth of my memory.
This story may be contsested
By people who remember it differently.
It is based on real people and real events
As I remember them.
My memory cannot be contested.
Truth cannot be broken.
Only hidden
Or shared.
This is my story
As I remember it.

For Big Dave...

By Little Dave.

Pre-Set

House-lights.

The stage is littered with tyres and batteries – exhausts and sparkplugs – spare parts of a Ford Escort – and Capri – the remains of a Fiat 126 – bits and bobs of various Vauxhalls and other spare parts belonging to other retro cars.

DAVID *(10) plays with the car parts as the audience enter.*

In between the selection and placement of car parts he says – 'And... And... And...'

*As the audience settle – the lights change and Michael Jackson's **"BAD"** album plays from the car radio.*

DAVID *makes himself a bed on a back seat and gets into it.*

He puts the headphones of his Walkman on and settles for sleep.

***"SMOOTH CRIMINAL"** plays – it rewinds – fast forwards – **"MAN IN THE MIRROR"** plays – it rewinds – fast forwards – **"THE WAY YOU MAKE ME FEEL"** plays – it rewinds – fast forwards – **"I JUST CAN'T STOP LOVING YOU"** plays – it rewinds – fast forwards – **"BAD"** plays – it slows down – like a Walkman on its last legs.*

As the batteries on David's Walkman die out – so do the lights and music.

Lights up.

---

* A licence to produce SPARKPLUG does not include a performance licence for "SMOOTH CRIMINAL", "MAN IN THE MIRROR", "THE WAY YOU MAKE ME FEEL", "I JUST CAN'T STOP LOVING YOU", "BAD" . For further information, please see Music Use Note on page v.

Prologue

DAVE *(35) enters.*

He talks over the following action.

He rearranges an item or two – tucking **DAVID** *into bed.*

He carefully removes the headphones and Walkman from the back seat and puts them away.

He rebuilds as much of the Ford Capri as possible.

DAVE

He's got two dads

My lad

One's black

That makes him

Black

I suppose

So I'm told.

He's got two dads

My lad

One's black

One's white

He's half-caste

They say

Others say

He's coloured

Some say

Mixed race.

He's got two dads

My lad

I've never met the

Black one

Or his others

His family

Sisters or brothers.

He's got two dads

My lad

The black

Keeps him distanced from

My family

That really bothers me.

He's got two dads

My lad

I want to hold him up

Show him to the world

Guide him through his

Mistakes

Stupidity

The only thing

The black one gave him was

Ethnicity.

He's got two dads

My lad

One played with him for hours

Days

Years

The other

Left when he was

Minus eight months old.

He's got two dads

My lad

One of them is hardly a

Man

Was never really his

The other was also

His mother

For a time.

He's got two dads

My lad

One is from Jamaica

His mother says

One of them is

The Greatest dad in the world

He says.

He's got two dads

My lad

One of them is his father

The other is just

A cock

With balls.

DAVE *gets into the car.*

He searches in the glove box – finds a tape – inserts it into the cassette player and presses play

1983.

*Rod Stewart's – **"TONIGHT'S THE NIGHT"** plays.**

** A licence to produce SPARKPLUG does not include a performance licence for "TONIGHT'S THE NIGHT". For further information, please see Music Use Note on page v.

DAVE sits in a car seat downstage – he holds the steering wheel/gearstick.

DAVE

So

Once again

Me

Inside

The car

Coming from

Irish Wythenshawe

Driving into

Moss Side with its

Ex-Island dwellers.

Outside of the car the bricks of the shops become a

Long

Red

Tunnel

Passing by my peripheral.

Inside of the car the smoke of a B&H gold

Blends with the soundtrack of a Rod Stewart

Knicker flicker
'STAY AWAY FROM MY WINDOW...
STAY AWAY FROM MY BACK DOOR TOO...
DISCONNECT THE TELEPHONE LINE...
RELAX BABY, DRAW THAT BLIND...'

Outside of the car is

Blurred

Just like my memory of it.

Dirty.

Inside of the car is me

Listening to proper heartbreakers

Smelling fresh

Looking sharp

As always.

I indicate

Outside of the car

Flashes of orange

A turn

Inside the car

A splash

A blending scent of Old Spice mixed with Holsten

A can of Pils plots its escape

It dives head-first towards the passenger side

'No'

I catch it

'Yes'

The car stalls

'Shit!'

Outside of the car

Is dark

Littered around the people are darker

Most of them moving with a rhythm

Talking in rhyme to a

Dumdumdumdumdidididumdumdummmm

Dumdumdumdumdidididumdumdummmm.

Inside the car

Keys turn

Everything rumbles

Thank fuck for that I'm thinking as

The tape cassette continues

My ears absorb the lyrics
'OOH BABY DON'T YOU HESITATE
'CAUSE
TONIGHT'S THE NIGHT'

I'm

Picking Angela up

Again

From her friend's place

As always.

I park up

Outside of the car is

Dark

Haze

Bass.

Inside the car

I'm sat

Waiting

Again

Looking at a flat above a barber's

A flat with a party inside

A flat that I know I could

You know

Get out

Knock on

Go up

Join in

Mam doesn't like Angela being alone in

These

Places

So I could

You know

Just be there

Just

Watch over like

You know.

But the atmosphere in there is not my

Cup of tea

Bottle of Diamond

Or can of Holsten

It's smoky thick with this dark bass.

You see they may fancy white on a woman's face but mine they'll

They could

People round here may think I'm a bit

You know

If I go up

Start

What am I trying to say?

I'm saying

I'm not one of those who are

Of the other

You know

Fear

I'm not scared

...

I'm from Wythenshawe

I'm hard

I've fought

Lots

I've beaten

Lots

I've been

I drive a belting Capri for fuck sake.

But

For some reason

Round here

It

Yeah it

Not because

Because they're

You know

I'm not one of them that thinks like that.

...

For fucksake she always does this

Says she'll be outside waiting when she's not

She's not there

Where she said she'll be

Again

She

She should be at home

With Craig

She should be

...

I hate it round here

It's too dark

It's...

It's just so dark

Round here

Moss Side.

Even on a clear blue day

The tight streets wrapped around the tall houses make everything a sort of

You know

With the steam from the brewery plus the smog from town it's like

Like

A maze of dark back alleys with no sunlight able to break through the smog thick clouds.

It's dodgy

Dodgy as fuck

Round here.

But

I'm Dave

I do the picking up.

Plus

Well

You know

Sisters have mates

Sometimes that mate is a real cracker

Who's going to need the best mate's brother with the Ford Capri to put things in the back of.

So

Yeah

Got my heart on Joanne

A little

She's

She's so

Into them

Their

That

Culture

You know

So

Yeah.

No go.

But

Still

I do

Just a little

She's

She's loud

She's different

She's

Yeah

She's not into me

I don't think

Not yet

But

Well

I've got the Capri so

We'll see

…

Where is she?

Come on Ange

She knows I hate wait—

—Outside the car

A couple of blokes

One of them with

Rastas?

Dreadlocks?

Anyway

They link up with these lads that have been waiting on the corner.

Inside the car

I remember

The locks

I've not locked the locks

The doors

You know what I mean?

For fuck sake

I can't just

Start

You know

Leaning over

Locking all the

Looks

I'd look like a

Like I'm hiding something.

Then

Outside the car

I see these lads again

But now it's a gang of 'em

Pointing up at Joanne's

Angela's at the window

I turn off Rod.

Inside the car

I can hear the shouting from

Outside the car.

I get out the car

It's Angela

She's screaming – *'Get off! Get the fuck off her, now!'*

Then

This

This fella appears at the window

He has Joanne by the hair

He's

He's holding her head out the window

...

Is that blood?

...

Is she bleeding?

...

Has he?

The fucking...

Now

I'm walking towards the barber's

Away from the car

Through a quartet of tutts from the gang

Followed by a

'Wotcha whitey'

I see the window's broke

Smashed

Has put her head through that?

As I get to the door

Further from my car
The party's parting
Most of the people leave
They disappear into the dark
I should
I should shout
Something
Call out
Find out what's going on
Find out who's smashed that window
Who's caused all this fucking drama
That's what I'd normally do
Never back down from a fight me
You know
But I do
I just let them pretend to ignore me
As if they can't see me sticking out like a fucking
Pigeon amongst cats.
Once they've gone
A cry from upstairs unfreezes me
So
I make my way in
Into
Into what seemed like the source of
All of the bass
All of the smoke.
I'm about
Four steps
Up the stairs

Towards Joanne

When a cough from the smoke

Becomes a choke from the bass as it shakes my lungs

...

I'm sprung into guard

As a

Fella

A man?

An Ainsley

I'll find out

Later

Anyway

He barges past me

Taking me

Two steps

Down

Away.

Before I have a chance to collar him

He goes.

Another moan

From upstairs

Takes me to the top of them

Straight into the living room

If you can call it that

Drugs everywhere

It stinks

Drinks spilt

Bits of glass from smashed bottles dance with splinters of window.

Some
Bob Marley wannabe
Sits on the floor
Sucking a
Druggy pipe.
Above him
A giant poster of the man himself
Laughing at me
With smoke in his mouth
Menace in his eyes.
I spot the record player
I grab it
I grab the druggy dosser
I show them both out the front door
From the top of the stairs
With a giant fucking
Smash.
Then
Quiet.
Then
Crying
Sobbing
Then
Somewhere in the smoke-stained shit
Joanne sits up
Soaked in tears
Covered in blood.
I try to calm myself
But it's like my heartbeat

Has replaced the bass beat

It shakes inside me.

As I move towards Joanne

I think of saying

It's alright?

I'm here?

Then a

Violent retch

From the toilet

Then again

Ange

Fucking hell.

I leave Joanne

With my thoughts of words that might've helped

Getting to Angela just in time to stop her drowning herself in the toilet

In her vomit

In her years of drunken mistreatment

...

'It's alright

I'm here'

...

In about ten minutes

Ange's out of the toilet

Joanne's out of her tears

But still in sobs

We're thirteen steps down

Outside of the barber's

Locking up Joanne's flat.

Then

Getting in

Into

Into the Capri

Taking Joanne to

Fallowfield.

Then taking

Ange

To Wythenshawe

To something familiar

To home

Where I'll get into telling my little sister a bit about herself

About her lack of

But

For now

It's

Quiet

Sort of

Joanne sobs in the front

Trying to

Trying

Ange slumps in the back

Trying to sleep

Whilst holding down her vomit.

She's a mess you know.

I pull up

After her one word since I found her

'Thanks'

Joanne's out of the car

Into her Grandparents'

...

'You can get in the front if you want Ange'
'Angela?!'

       'What Dave?'

'You can get in the front'

       'I'm alright here Dave'

'Get in the front'

       'I don't feel well Dave'

'Stop taking drugs then'

       What? There weren't any
       drugs Dave.
       Don't be daft'

'There was. I could smell them Ange.
Fucking Druggies' pipes everywhere'

       'It's just a bit of weed Dave.
       Can we go home please?'

...

I decide to keep quiet for a sec
She looks like she could throw up any minute

...

Not in the Capri mate
No fucking way

...

Half way home
She starts to make a recovery
Miraculously
Brush out of her bag
On her hair

Perfume out

Sprayed

On her sick

'You can't keep on like this you know'

'I know Dave yeah'

'They'll take Craig for good'

'I know Dave yeah'

'So?'

'I know Dave yeah'

'Are you listening to me Ange?'

'Yeah Dave yeah'

With that

That

Attitude

I give up

Not completely but

I'm not

I can't be her

Her dad

It's not

I

I don't want her to hate me for

For telling her the truth

I haven't got the right.

What could I tell her anyway?

She can't cope

She needs help with Craig

She can't stay with Mam anymore

It's killing her

Mam's

...

Before I've parked the Capri

Ange's out

In through the back door

Into bed

Soon to be in Mam's hands.

I take the tax disc out

Put it in the glove box

I lock up the Capri

Unlock the front door

Then enter a house

A home

That I shouldn't be the

Man of.

I get in

Into bed

Into

DAVE *leans into the car.*

He presses play on the cassette player.

1983

UB40's – ***"BRING ME YOUR CUP"*** *plays.****

*** A licence to produce SPARKPLUG does not include a performance licence for "BRING ME YOUR CUP". For further information, please see Music Use Note on page v.

DAVE

Into

Joanne's life

I'm in

She's in

We're in my car

The Capri

I knew it'd come good.

Me

Joanne

The car

Me

Joanne

A drive

A drive here

A drive there

We can go

Anywhere.

I'm about to tell her how much

How far I'd actually go for her

When she says

> *'I'm pregnant. That's... That's
> why he did it.*
>
> *Ainsley. He didn't think it was
> his so he...he...'*

...

That's what happened

At the party

That shit pot put her head through the window because

Because

The fucking shithead

I'll

I'll

'I'm here, you know. Whatever you need

You know I... I like you Joanne. A lot.

Whatever you. I've got the car. Whenever.

Wherever. It's alright. I'm here'

Then it's just

Me

For Joanne.

Me

Wanting her.

Wanting her badly.

Me

Joanne.

Me

Joanne

In

We're in

We're

Constantly being interrupted by the—

'In-ter-rup-ting?

That's a long word for you innit Dave?'

'Fuck off Ange, you are'

'She's not interrupting me'

'Thanks Joanne'

'What time does Paul finish?'

'Six. I think'

'Right. Get in then. I'll drop you off'

'It's only just gone five'

'Yeah, well, you can wait outside for him'

'Can't you. Get in'

Before she can get anymore in the way

The Capri has whipped us through

Moss Side with its

Red-bricked tunnels

In

Then out of

Chorlton-cum-Hardy with its

Green drunkenness

Into

Wild Wythenshawe with its

Never ending community

Dumping Angela

Out

Leaving her at the side of

Paul's work.

Where she will sit

For over two hours

Waiting

For the worst thing to ever happen to her.

Paul.

She met him a couple weeks ago

We met him

Me

Joanne

Angela.

I'd convinced them to stop knocking about in Moss Side

Come for a drink with me round here

Round my way.

So

We're sat in

The Hanging Chandelier

Me

Joanne

Angela.

This Paul

He's stood over the way

Stuffing the jukebox with 10p's.

It responds by coughing up all these

Irish songs.

Me mam's favourites.

Before you know it

Angela's attending all his attention seeking

This Paul.

He's not my kind a bloke

Loud

Foul

Trouble.

But I

I should have seen then

Kept an eye on Angela

Looked over her

You know

But

Well

I had Joanne to entertain.

I was looking at Joanne

She was looking at me

Then it's just

Us again.

Me

Wanting her again.

Wanting her

To get close.

Closer.

To me.

To let me

In

Into

Into

DAVE *gets into the car and changes the music on the cassette player.*

He turns the engine on. He presses play.

1983.

*Rod Stewart's – **"DO YA THINK I'M SEXY"** plays.* ****

DAVE *gets out and sits on the bonnet/boot of the car.*

DAVE

Then we're kissing

Then we're hugging

Then we're holding hands

Then we're waking up.

**** A licence to produce SPARKPLUG does not include a performance licence for "DO YOU THINK I'M SEXY". For further information, please see Music Use Note on page v.

Then we're in the Capri

We're in shops

We're buying baby things

We're making baby plans

We're telling family that

'We're having a baby'

Then we go for check ups

Then we find out

'It's a boy'

Then we're naming him after me

Then we're naming him after you

Then we piss Mam off

We look for a place

We move into our house

We have a garden in the front

We have a garden in the back

We have a garage on the side.

There's a school around the corner

There's a chance

'We could really make a go of it here'

But we're still pissing Mam off

But now we're close

We're really close

We're about to meet little

David

Little David Judge

But we're really

We're really

We are really pissing my Mam off

But I

I don't know why

I don't know why she

Why she can't just—

– *The engine cuts out.*

Music stops.

Lights change.

Then we're in

We're on

It's on

It's happening

It's all fucking

Go

Go

Go.

I help Joanne

Waters broke an' all

Into the Capri.

Pre-towelled

Un-smoked.

Joanne gets in

Lights a fag.

Then we're in the car

It's moving but

But I'm not driving

Well

I am

Of course I am.

I'm in the front

Joanne's in the back

Windows open

Hair flying

Smoke fuming

David coming

DAVID *'And?'*

That's it

I'm not driving.

I'm not driving because

Just driving

No aim

Nowhere to go

No one to be

I'm not that now.

Right now it's

It's

Changed

Forever

Now I'm going somewhere

I'm going to the hospital

DAVID *'And?'*

I'm going to see David

DAVID *'And?'*

I'm going to be a dad

I'm going to be his

His...

That was

This

I mean

I love Joanne

Of course I do

To bits

But that's not the love I feel now

Now

Already

Before he's even here

Before he

He

You know?

I know now right now

It

It smacks me straight in the face.

I know I'm going to be his dad

David's dad

Even if the colour of his skin is different to mine

I've got no choice but to be there for him

Always.

Then

Then I'm thinking forward

Beyond the hospital

Past the nappies

Past all that shit

After kicking the ball in the park

Teaching him to ride his bike

Just there

Somewhere in the smell after the fresh baby

The mucky kid

Somewhere there

Or just after

My lad's gonna want to know his

Dad

His other one

His proper one

His

Black one.

I remember Mam with her foul words

> *'What do you want that slag's*
> *black problem for?'*

...

The car parks itself outside the hospital

The memory leaves me.

Joanne

The baby

Joanne's having a baby

Our baby.

We're having a baby.

Fucking porter bloke walks past

'Ey mate'

> *'What mate?'*

'Baby. We've got. She's having it.'

> *'Congrats mate'*

'Now'

> *'Right'*

'Well get a fucking wheelchair then'

Fucking Dickhead.

'You alright Joanne?'

Of course she is

Hardly broke a sweat

Wants another fag

So we sit there

Smoking

Waiting.

For a second I forget what's going on

INHALE

I'm enjoying this fag

EXHALE

Really enjoying this

INHALE

E

X

H

A

L

E

Then knob-head comes back with a wheelchair just as a

'AAAAHHHH ... FUCK!'

Scares the life out of him.

Joanne puts herself in the chair

I push her in

Into the hospital

Into

DAVE *leans into the car and turns the keys.*

Lights change.

1984.

Radio plays.

DAVE *washes the car.*

DAVE
> This car's not my first
> Won't be my last
> Not my worst or best.
> All my cars are never
> Brand new
> They all belonged to someone else before
> You know.
> But
> David
> He's mine
> My only
> Ever.
> Not blood
> But fuck blood
> He's my soul
> My heart
> My get out of bed for.
> But Mam
> Like many mams out there
> Wants
> Wanted
> A new one.
> A new one?
> They're all new

Aren't they?

New to me.

She wants me to have

Mine

From me

From Her

From.

I've got David

But Mam's one of them that sees brown as

As

Something hard to call

Hers

Her own.

She's not

You know

She loves black people

It's not that

It's just

Well

She's Irish

Old school

Proud

You know

Proper proud.

I think she wouldn't be happy unless I married

Mary – Josephine – Orla – Maeve – Teresa – Mafuckin-Guire.

So when I proposed to

'Joanne'

Who got knocked up by that

'Dark fella'

I could see it

The worry

In her eyes

The fear.

That's the same fear I saw in her when I came out of that maternity room with David in my arms.

...

I was the first

To hold him.

After the doctor did

You know?

What he does

I held him before Joanne

She was out of it

Over eight pounds he was.

...

Happiest day of my life

...

I remember all the faces

Everyone's

Joanne's grandparents.

My mam's

Sour.

Angela's

Paul's

Craig with the Opal Fruits

A big family bag of Opal Fruits.

He's not daft Craig

All of four years old now

Four years of being passed around

Fending for himself

He's a clever lad

Knew babies weren't born with teeth

Too right he should eat 'em

> *'I thought it was the thought that counts'*

'It is Craig. Don't worry'

I remember Paul

Snatching them off him.

Slowly sucking them in front of him

One by one

For the rest of the day.

I forgot about that

He's a snide bastard.

But I couldn't see it then

Only saw Angela in love with him

Craig with a mum

A

Home

At last.

I remember Angela

At ours

Planning happy families.

Then Joanne

At Mam's

Planning family holidays.

More Sunday dinners

At ours.

Mam biting her tongue.

That was it

That was us

The next generation

With the next generation

Moving forward

Moving

In

Into

DAVE *enters the car – as he exits through the other side the car seems to transform.*

1985/6.

Over the following text – **DAVE** *applies the finishing touches to his new second-hand Ford Escort.*

Into the new car

For the new things

The good things

All the

Things.

Joanne's got her home

Her plans.

I

Me

I've got it all

Everything

The makings of a proper fucking family.

Family

Family

We lose one

They gain two

Angela has twins

Natalie then Patrick

Craig's new responsibility.

...

We

Were

Decorating walls

Sorting out the garden

Front

Back

Cleaning out the garage

On the side

        'Should we get a dog Dave?

        We should get a dog

        We've got the space'

'Let's get a dog'

        'Yeah?'

'Yeah'

        'Yes'

So we do

Paddy.

'Paddy... Sit'

David loves him

They love each other.

Paddy has this

Smile

David's got this

Laugh

Like a little machine-gun

'A-A-A-A-A-A-A-A-A-A-A-A-A'

He doesn't stop

Laughing

Growing

Laughing at all sorts.

Learning.

He knows more than you think

He walks

He talks

He laughs at Joanne's dirty jokes

Laughs at anyone's jokes

Dirty or not.

With this laugh

Like a little

This

'A-A-A-A-A-A-A-A-A-A-A-A-A-A-A'

Craig ducks for cover whenever he hears it

Pretends he's in the Vietnam War

'Incoming! ...Incoming'

Puts this daft American accent on

'Incoming'

Gets David every time

'A-A-A-A-A-A-A-A-A-A-A-A-A-A-A'

Then Craig gets shot

'Goes down

'UH'

In slow motion

'UH – UH'

Like

Proper Platoon

'UH – UH – UH'

David can't stop

'A-A-A-A-A-A-A-A-A-A

A-A-A-A-A-A-A-A-A-A

A-A-A-A-A-A-A-A-A-A'

Then everyone's at it

Falling about

Living room full of dead bodies due to David's deadly machine-gun laugh.

It's

You know

It's fun

Proper fun

We have loads of it.

Until he gets

You know

Gets carried away

David.

He gets very

Excitable

Very easily.

Always wants more

At four

It's

More

More

More.

He wants

Laughs

He wants

Attention

Us

He wants his mum

'Mum

Mum

Mum

Mum

Mum'

But she

She doesn't

He bounces off the walls

It

You know

He

Sends her up 'em.

So

I

I just try to

Make it fun

Keep us happy

You know.

I'm not gonna go shouting or

Smacking him or anything.

I can't can I

I'm

He's not

Something on the car breaks – tyre burst or engine smoke.

DAVE *chooses to ignore it.*

There was this time

He must have been

Two

Just

...

Yeah

He was helping Joanne

With the cleaning

He loves the Hoover

Henry

Holds the wire for Joanne.

His best bit is when she's finished

He gets to wind the wire in

You know

Back in

With the thing

The

The Winder inny thing.

Anyway

I'd just finished in the kitchen with this

This flat pack

Stack of shelving

Was a pain in the arse.

I'd been shouting

But they couldn't hear me

Both caught up in their fascination of cleaning.

Both singing along to the

UB40

Pumping out from Joanne's stereo.

Joanne sings.

'Give me your bottle. I've got a cup. We'll pop the cork then take a sup...'

David shouts.

'GIVE ME... A BOTTLE. I GOT...A CUP...POP PORK THEN TIE UP...'

...

Someone'll love a tryer

...

So

So I've finished putting together this

Flat pack

Stack of shelves.

They can't hear me.

So I think

Right

I'll have 'em.

This bottle of ketchup's been sitting there

On the side

Staring at me for the past half hour.

So I pop it open

Plop a load of it

On me chest

Over my white vest

Looks proper

Horror show

You know?

Gruesome.

I grab a knife from the drawer

Put it under me armpit.

I crawl

All fours

Into the living room.

Acting all

Dying

Almost dead

But they don't notice me

They're investigating some sort of super dust in the corner.

So I drag myself towards them

Grab Joanne's heel

'Urrrrrgggghhh. Help me Joanne'

She jumps out of her skin

'AAAARRGGHHH'

David goes white

I start laughing

Joanne's starts shouting

'Fucking hell Dave.'

I'm still laughing

Can't help it.

Then David walks up to me

Starts hitting my knee with Henry's bendy bit.

He goes

He shouts

'Fucking hell Dad!'

...

Everything stops.

Silence.

He's standing there

Little David

Face full of chub

Arms folded over his belly

Looking at me with this

This frown

Stern

Old

Older than he looks

'What?'

'What?'

'What did you just say to your dad?'

'Nothing'

I burst out pissing myself

Couldn't help it

He only did what his mum did

Told me off

Proper.

I'd scared him

His little face

It was like that

'What you talking about Willis?'

That

Him.

Anyway

Before you know it we're all rolling around

Laughing our heads off

Taking cover from David's

'A-A-A-A-A-A-A-A-A'

Yeah.

Then watching Joanne's face as she saw the ketchup

Everywhere

On the floor

The couch

A big fucking trail of it through to the kitchen

'It's always a step too far'

'It's alright Joanne. We'll get a new couch'

'That was new Dave'

'It's second hand. Cushions don't even match.

'That's not the point Dave'

'We'll get another Joanne. Relax.

Should have got a new one in the first place'

'You sound like your mam'

'What?'

'You heard'

'Fuck off Joanne!'

That was the first time I snapped at her

I think.

Yeah

It was

Made David cry

Poor lad.

If you thought his laugh was bad

His cry was

It

...

There was this other occasion

Time

Not too long ago

With this fucking

That shitty flat pack of shelves.

He'd started nursery

Reception?

One of them.

Quite the little

Man of the house now

Little David

Up early

Making his own breakfast

Well

Trying to

We don't let him

Not here

But

Angela

Paul

They don't wake up until

I don't know

Two

Three pm

Ever.

We've been letting David stay there

At weekends

Give Joanne

Give us both a bit of

Space

Time.

When he's there he's got Craig

Natalie

Patrick

They keep each other

Occupied

You know

Play together

Not wanting

Demanding all the time.

Sounds daft but

Just one

Bit of a handful.

Anyway

He's up

Watching

His *Thriller* video

Loved Michael Jackson

Wanted to be him.

Still does.

So

He's downstairs

In the living room

Me

Jo

We're upstairs

In bed

We're usually up at six

For the stall

So it must have been early.

We both jump awake

Straight out of our skin when we hear this

This

Bang

Thud

Crash

A sort of

Bomb

Yeah

Sounded like a bomb

In the kitchen.

Then

We hear it.

David

Crying.

This sound

I'd never felt anything like it.

Before I knew it I was

Out of bed

Down the stairs

Into the kitchen

In what felt like

One breath.

Two steps.

As Jo arrives behind me

I pull the re-flat packed stack of shitty shelves off

'David!'

He's covered in blood!

Quick Joanne!

Fucking

The ambulance

We' –

                                 – *'It's fucking Ketchup Dave!'*

'What?'

                                 'This is not funny David! Do you hear me?!

                                 Stop crying. Listen to me!'*

None of us were laughing

Me or David

We were both shit scared.

I was

I was so fucking happy it was ketchup.

Joanne was livid

Blaming me for playing too much

                                 'You can't always be his friend. You've got to be a parent as well Dave. It's not fair'

She thought he was lying

Playing pranks like his dad.

He wanted a bowl of Sugar Puffs

So he climbed up to get them.

It's fair enough

It's not his fault the shelves are made of shit.

I know

He's not allowed to be making his own but

We've been leaving him with Ange haven't we

With Craig.

Probably fending for themselves

Foraging through the mess like a pack of

Manky meerkat cubs.

So

...

Yeah

When he got to the top

Where the Sugar Puffs were

The shelves started to fall back

Off the cabinet

Taking David

The Sugar Puffs

Plus

An open bottle of ketchup

Onto the floor

One after another

With a bang

A thud

A crash

Then the crying

The panicking

The shouting

The telling off

The smacking

Not me but

But

...

Yeah

What could I do?

...

Find myself saying that a lot

'What can I do Jo?'

> *'Why's it always me Dave?'*

'I can't hit him can I?'

> *'Why's that Dave?'*

'Why's what?'

> *'Do you want to be his Dad or his friend?'*

'I am his Dad. Don't be daft'

> *'Are you sure about that Dave?'*

...

We got rid of them shelves

...

Built some fitted ones

...

DAVE *removes flat pack shelves from the stage and exits.*

1988.

Butlins.

COMPERE *(voiceover)*

> *'Boys*
>
> *Girls*
>
> *Mums*
>
> *Dads*
>
> *Put your hands together*
>
> *Welcome to the stage*
>
> *David Judge'*

DAVID *(5) enters.*

*He presses play on the car radio – Michael Jackson's
"BAD" plays.******

DAVID *starts to dance along to the music – as if he is
Jacko.*

DAVID *continues dancing with the music.*

> *'David is...?*
>
> *Five years old.*
>
> *He's from...?*
>
> *Manchester.'*

'Whoooops' from the crowd.

> *'Thank you*
>
> *Thank*
>
> *You.*
>
> *David's here with...?*
>
> *All of his family.*
>
> *They're here for...?*
>
> *One week.*
>
> *So far David has enjoyed...?*
>
> *Playing on the arcade machines with his big
> cousin Craig the most.*
>
> *David thinks he can win the Michael Jackson
> dance-off because he's...?*
>
> *Michael's biggest fan in the whole wide world*
>
> *Also...*
>
> *His Dad says he's a...*
>
> *A better dancer than Craig'*

***** A licence to produce SPARKPLUG does not include a
performance licence for "BAD". For further information, please
see Music Use Note on page v.

Laughter from the crowd.

> **'So**
>
> **Dancing to**
>
> **'Bad'**
>
> **Please put your hands together**
>
> **Make some noise for**
>
> **David Judge'**

A long applause as – DAVID finishes his routine – collects his trophy.

The music ends.

The applause fades as – DAVID moonwalks off the stage.

Lights change.

Day becomes night.

MUSIC: "EYE OF THE TIGER"****** – Starts

A change in the atmosphere – from family friendly to adult only (ish).

DAVE *enters.*

He's topless.

DAVE *moves through a series of pressups and poses.*

He 'fireman lifts' an audience member up and carries them around the stage.

After a lap or two he places them back in their seat.

****** A licence to produce SPARKPLUG does not include a performance licence for "EYE OF THE TIGER". For further information, please see Music Use Note on page v.

He moves towards the largest object on the stage.

COMPERE *(voiceover)*

> '*The winner*
> *Of*
> *Mr Butlins*
> *Pwllheli*
> *1988*
> *Is*
> *Drum roll please*'

The crowd roll drums on the tables and stamp their feet.

> '*Is...*'

DAVE *struggles but eventually lifts the object above his head.*

> '*...Dave Judge*'

The crowd cheers.

> '*Dave*
> *Congratulations.*
> *Come on*
> *Put that down.*
> *A few words*
> *How does it feel to be*
> *Mr Butlins Pwllheli 88?*'

'Great
It feels great
Yeah'

> '*Well*
> *That's great.*
> *Here's your trophy*

> *You can take that home with you'*

'Thanks'

DAVE *collects his trophy.*

> *'We can engrave it*
> *With your name on*
> *Only a fiver'*

'Yeah

I will

Do that

Thanks

Yeah'

> *'Don't forget your crisp*
> *Spend on what you want*
> *Twenty pound note'*

'Whoops' from the crowd.

'Yep

Thanks'

> *'Ladies*
> *Gentlemen*
> *Put your hands together'*

'Sorry

Can I just say

One thing?'

> *'Just a second please*
> *Quiet down now*
> *Mr Butlins 88 has something he wants to say'*

'Thanks

I just want to erm

Thank my wife

Joanne.

As well as my lad

David.

I want to erm

He won the Michael Jackson Dance so

Yeah I'm made up

We both' –

        – *'Your son?'*

'David

Yeah'

        'The one that's...

        The winner?'

'Yeah'

        'But he was...'

'What?'

        'The half-caste one?'

'Yes

David Judge'

        'So...?'

'So

What?'

        'So

        Sorry

        I didn't

        Mr Butlins ladies

        Gentlemen'

COMPERE – *voiceover ends.*

DAVE *rearranges objects/car parts.*

He is now sat in a caravan with family.

DAVE –.

'So

So who the fuck is he

Prick

Tosser

I'll…

        'Calm down Dave. Have another drink'

'No Angela

No

As if I'm not his Dad

Fucking

Did you see his face?

Did you see his face Joanne?'

        'Yeah, I'll have one Angela'

        'Grab that bottle there Paul'

'One more look like that

I swear to God

I won't have it'

        *'Yeah, he was asking for it. I'd
have nutted him. Here you're
Dave'*

        *'Must've thought you were
fucking one of them. Blown
his mind'*

'Yeah

What?'

        'Pass them around then Paul'

        'What are you saying Paul?'

        'Nothing Jo. Just, you know'

'*No. I don't. What?*'

'**Anyway**

I won

We both won'

'**Cheers**'

They drink.

Quiet.

...

> '*The fella was right. Really. Not right but...*
>
> *You know? It's not normal is it? Really?*
>
> *You're bound to get looks. Lots. Like his. Really.*
>
> *Plus they're not lying. Are they? Really? I mean...*
>
> *It's not yours. Is it Dave? Not really. You're going to have to face that. At some point...*
>
> *Really.*'
>
> '*Fuck off Nancy!*'

'**Joanne**'

...

That was

That

Was

Was what it was like every time we went to Butlins.

Every year.

Rows

Fights

Falling outs.

The kids were alright

Hardly saw them

Off

Playing

Only came back for food

Money for the arcade.

It was us

We were the problem

The adults.

The drink

On top of the

Misery

Spite

Bitterness

Anger.

I just wanted it simple

Everything simple

Easy

Safe

Smooth

Smooth

Music –.

It slows down – like a Walkman on its last legs.

He rearranges an item or two – tucking **DAVID** *into bed.*

1989.

Bedtime was

It was beautiful to be honest

At the end.

Nightmarish

At the start.

Before

'Bedtime'

The key is to get him into bed before he remembers

'The Bill'

It's Craig's favourite programme

So it's

David's favourite programme.

As soon as he hears the music

He's up

Walking the beat

Marching around the living room

'Duddun – Duddun – Dun'

He's funny.

But

Eight o' clock is his bedtime

He's only six

Nearly seven but

Thinks he's as old as Craig sometimes.

The fights

The wars he has with Jo if he can't stay up to watch it

It's

It's out of order really.

But everything he says

He's heard from us

The swearing

The temper.

'This is why he's up

Bouncing around all the time'

>   *'It's got warm milk in it Dave'*

'So?'

>   *'So it puts you to sleep doesn't it? Warm*
>   *milk.'*

'Not with coffee in it Joanne, no'

>   *'What are you trying to say Dave?'*

'What am I trying to say?'

>   *'Yes. Are you deaf? What are you*
>   *saying?'*

'I'm saying

You shouldn't give him coffee

Before he goes to bed'

>   *'I know how to get my son to bed Dave'*

...

So

...

So anyway

If we do

Get him to bed

Before

'*The Bill*'

It's fine

He's fine.

He puts his Walkman on

Falls asleep listening to that.

We have a few drinks

Nice early night

Ready to wake up early

Pack the stall

Off to the market.

Smooth

Happy

Just how I want it.

But the best bit

My best

Thing

Is

Just before we go to bed.

I check in on David

Makes sure he hasn't

Hasn't

Strangled himself or anything

You know

With his headphones

Anyway

He never has

Always sound asleep.

I can hear his Walkman

Somewhere in bed with him

Battery dying.

So I find it

Take his headphones off him

Replace them with a kiss.

Then

Wait for it

Then I put the headphones to my ear

Most times

Most times it's Michael Jackson

But

Sometimes

Every so often

It's Rod.

He's been listening to Rod Stewart.

That's my best bit.

My best thing.

So far.

...

The car stereo comes to life.

"SMOOTH CRIMINAL" *plays – it rewinds – fast forwards –* **"MAN IN THE MIRROR"** *plays – it rewinds – fast forwards –* **"THE WAY YOU MAKE ME FEEL"** *plays – it rewinds – fast forwards –* **"I JUST CAN'T STOP LOVING YOU"** *plays – it rewinds – fast forwards –* **"BAD"** *plays.* *******

DAVE *carefully removes the headphones and Walkman from the back seat. He presses stop.*

DAVE *re-arranges another car.*

It's smaller – very small.

******* A licence to produce SPARKPLUG does not include a performance licence for "SMOOTH CRIMINAL", "MAN IN THE MIRROR", "THE WAY YOU MAKE ME FEEL", "I JUST CAN'T STOP LOVING YOU", "BAD". For further information, please see Music Use Note on page v.

It's a Fiat 126.

He gets into the passenger seat.

DAVE *takes a breath.*

*The car starts – UB40 – **"BRING ME YOUR CUP"**********
plays on the stereo.*

DAVE *turns the volume down.*

Low.

The windscreen wipers squeal in the rain.

DAVE

'A fucking... 126?'

        'Yeah. What?'

'Come on Joanne'

        'What?'

'We can't go to the market in this'

        'Why not?'

'It's a Fiat 126'

        'So?'

'So how're we gonna fit the stall in that Joanne?'

        *'It fits. I've tried it. Shut up about it
now.'*

Windscreen wipers.

'Tax? MOT?'

        'It was fifty quid Dave'

'Yeah. Well.'

'Well what?'

'Just let me deal with cars in the future'

'This car's mine Dave.'

Windscreen wipers.

That's got a smell to it that hasn't it?

Mine?

Windscreen wipers.

'Right?'

'Right. So there'll be plenty of space once you've got yours back'

'Space?'

'...For the stock. For the stall... There'll be space on the passenger seat'

'What. So we take both cars?'

'Yeah'

'Both?'

'Yeah. I'll take mine. You take yours.'

'Right'

Windscreen wipers.

Something stinks

It stinks as shit this fucking Fiat.

Windscreen wipers.

Both?

Two cars?

Why do we need that?

Why does she want that?

I've got the Sierra

I do the

I drive

I do the driving

I've always drove

That's what I do

That's how I help

With my car

I've always had

The car

That's what I know

Cars.

Then I realised what I could smell

I think she was

You know

She was

It felt like

It smelt like she was getting ready to

Leave.

Leave me

Windscreen wipers.

I couldn't clear this smell off me

It clung to me for the rest of that day

The next

The week's worth

DAVE *gets out of the car.*

He slowly but surely snaps the windscreen wipers off the car.

He gets back into the car.

The passenger side.

Another day

We get back

Back to the house

Inside the car is cramped

Stinks.

Outside the car David's sat there

On the door step

The front door step

The car's lights turn off

Just in time to save David from becoming the rabbit.

As he looks up

He's in a right state

Tears everywhere

Glass on the floor.

I get out of the car

I can hear it

His cry.

By now he's got a couple of different cries David

He's got like that fucking

World war bomb warning one

When they want something that they can't have but they can't accept it so they work themselves into such a state that the cry is kind of stuck on a

You know the one.

There's the one where he's hurt himself

Like the Sugar Puffs

With the shelf

The flat pack

You know

That hurts your heart as soon as you hear it.

But none of them are this one

This is the

He's

Sorry

He

Didn't

He's

Really

Really sorry

But he

Was

Playing with a brick.

The sort of end of the initial shock crying

Time to get myself out of the shit intake of breath before the end of each word crying

You know the one.

He was just

Throwing

It

The brick

In

In the air

His wrist

The brick was heavy

So.

Now Joanne sees the broken glass panel in the front door

Poor David's shitting himself.

So

So

So his hand

Wrist

Slipped

The

The

The brick

Went through

The glass.

As he gets them last words out

He curls up into a ball on the doorstep

He knows

We both know

Exactly what's coming for him

Then Joanne shouts at him

Smacks him through the front door

Into the house

Into

The exhaust drops from the bottom of the car.

DAVE *ignores it.*

Into

1990.

DAVE

David getting harder to handle.

Getting into playing out.

Getting into scraps

With other kids.

Getting into whatever he can get into wherever he can get into it.

I can remember that first knock on the door.

Parents knocking because he had his first fight

On his walk home from school

Before

Earlier that day.

They knocked twice

The second louder.

Then I'm at the door all proud

Full of

'What's your problem pal?'

They see

A.C.A.B

All coppers are bastards

Shared amongst four of my ten knuckles.

Nothing buckles

They don't back down

I'm a racist

Is their presumption

Doubled

By the four eyes

Two yellowed

Scorching my features.

Then Joanne joins

Then the four of us stare

White inside

Black out there –   *'Where is... David?'*

Are you his father?

The other –   **'Hmmmm! No wonder he speak
                   that evil.**

                   **You encourage him say such
                   foul things?**

                   Is that you?'

I'm speechless

I'm

Am I his father?

Fuck me

For a moment

I thought he was

They were

His family.

David's.

You know

His

Black one.

But it's not

It wasn't.

Then its

They're all –   **'Our daughter. Monique.**
                   Should not be suffering abuse.
                   **Or attacks. On her way home from
                   school.'**

The other –   **'This is not the seventies. We
                   could call police'**

'Hold on.

What's happened?'

                   'Your boy.

David.

Where is he?

The racist thug.'

'You need to watch your mouth now mate.

Tell me what's happened?'

'What happen is. Your boy. This... David.

Has beat on our daughter Monique.

Calling her nigga this. Nigga that!'

'David?'

'Yes! That the boy!'

'David!'

'A second of silence then.'

He's at the door.

Then their faces.

Their faces

Fuck me it was almost funny.

My racist this?

My racist that?

My evil boy?

They're looking at little brown David

Full of puppy fat.

Slumped over like

Like SadSack

Stood between the two of us.

Both as white as the racists they took us for.

Their faces now look

They look

Sorry?

Guilty?

More.

Confused.

David says

He knows no different.

He's not...

To him

Fat equals fatty.

Spots equals spotty.

Smelly equals

Piss the bed Jed.

Ginger equals ginger nut.

Black equals nigga.

Brown equals Paki.

He gets called that a lot.

That's what they say he says.

Just kids in school.

Now

Now they are embarrassed.

They can see we haven't told him.

He hasn't asked

Hasn't needed to

Joanne's his mum

Dave's his dad

Full stop.

But he's cleverer than he looks

David

He figured it out whilst they were standing there.

His chubby brown skin

His short curls.

I wouldn't dare

You know

Tell him.

I could

I'll lose him if I do.

So I don't

Let him know he has another

That looks like them.

Him

Out there.

But I can't keep that from him

Can I?

Just because I'm

I've

...

DAVE *drags the exhaust from under the car.*

He attempts to repair it.

DAVE

Then

Then into

The hard stuff

The shit stuff

The who has rights to what

The who's giving up the most

The who's given the most

The

'I'm not letting him go without a fucking fight!'

DAVE *dismantles the cars carefully.*

He places parts of the Fiat on one side.

Parts of the Sierra on the other side.

The back seats remain untouched.

1991.

DAVE

He's sat there

Six in the morning

Every morning

Watching telly

Watching the Turtles or...

He didn't have a clue what was coming

'Let's ask him then?'

'Ask him what?'

'Who he wants to live with'

'Are you being serious?

He's eight years old!'

'I am serious Dave. He's my fucking son!'

'You what?'

'You heard.

Whoever he doesn't choose can fuck off out of here'

'Where you going?

Joanne

Don't!'

DAVE *runs off the stage.*

DAVID *enters.*

He picks and places car parts.

In between the selection and placement of car parts he says – 'And... And... And...'

He has rebuilt.

...

The Ford Sierra.

He sits in the car and presses play on the cassette player.

Michael Jackson – **"JUST GOOD FRIENDS"********** *– plays from the stereo – loud.*

1991/92

DAVE *gets out of the car and shouts over the music.*

He chose me.

He

Chose

Me.

He chose me because

Because

Because

I was his mate?

I was his wrestling partner?

I was his partner in crime?

******** A licence to produce SPARKPLUG does not include a performance licence for "JUST GOOD FRIENDS". For further information, please see Music Use Note on page v.

But he didn't pick his mum

Didn't pick her because

Because she disciplined him?

I didn't.

Because she made him eat his dinner?

I let him leave it.

He picked me because

Because

Because I love him more.

Yes.

I do.

That's why

DAVE *turns the music down.*

Then over the next year it wasn't about

Us

Me

Joanne

Me Joanne the stall

Me Joanne the split.

It was about David

School

School gates

Playing with mates.

Me

David

Playing footy

Eating egg fried rice with curry

Seeing Mam

Eating boiled ham with cabbage.

Weekends with Craig

Paul

Ange

The twins.

Picking him up from school

Waiting at the gate

Monday.

Football

Tuesday.

More school

Football after school.

David's mates.

Coming in late.

Starts fighting more

Leaving eight

Almost nine years old

Never starts the fights

But he's in them most the time.

More kids

Less mates

More questions

School gates

A few romances

Dates in the diary

It's rare to see a man like me

Single parent with a brown lad

You know

I am Mr nineteen-fucking-ninety.

Then teachers can't teach

So I do what I can

Teaching him how to

Stick up for himself

Right from wrong

Hit the biggest one first

They won't bother again.

But he will get bother

He's an half-caste kid with a white Dad

White mother

Wherever she is

...

I miss her

I miss

> *'So listen right now yeah. Now yeah. Just been*
> *dentist innit. Dint have to come back till after*
> *lunch innit. So have you seen that programme*
> *The Time, The Place. It's on in the day innit.*
> *Yeah. The Time, The Place.*

I saw her on the telly

Joanne

The show with that

Kilroy in it

Some

Daytime talk show pile of

> *'His mum was on it. Guess go on guess what.*
> *You'll never believe it eeew his mum is nasty*
> *man. Pure nasty. Check what she said yeah*
> *now yeah. She said.'*

The

The title of the episode

Show

Whatever it is

The title was

I'm a Gay Mum

Or something stupid like that

> *'She was sat there with aww nah man. Check now yeah she was sat with her girlfriend innit. I swear down now yeah her. Her girlfriend.'*

She was with this other one

Another gay

Lesbian

Mandy

Her

Girlfriend

> *'Pure nasty that innit. Dirty that. I'm gonna batter him for that you know. I should innit. We should batter him for that innit. His mum's nasty man pure nasty man. Can't get away with that can he. No way*
>
> *No way man*
>
> *Eyar*
>
> *Eeeew*
>
> *You're nasty you*
>
> *Nasty family you*
>
> *Gay you*
>
> *Gay boy you*
>
> *Bumboy you*
>
> *Aren't ya*
>
> *Go on admit it*
>
> *Batty man*
>
> *Must be if your mum is*

Your nasty lezza mum

Lesbo gay mum

Nasty you

How were you even born?

What the fuck are you?

Little Paki gay boy

African bum cleaner

Come on then

What

Come on

What

Eeew

Get away from me

Who you looking at

Lezbo lover

What you gonna do

What you gonna fucking do

Fight!

Fight!

FIGHT!

FIGHT!!

FIGHT!!!'

Car alarm goes berserk.

...

I'll never forget the day when he came

The cig outside

My doubts

The hospital

The smell

The love

The blood

The cry

His cry

Him

The promise I made to both of yers

To be there for him like

Like I had you

To be like you

A

Dad.

I was happy again

I felt connected to you

To life

To everything.

My love for everything changed in a way I didn't know it could

But

But that

That

Happiest day of my life

Has always been tainted by that look of fear in Mam's eyes

Never forget that.

Now

Eight years later

Standing at the door

Waiting for what feels like

Permission

To enter my own mother's house

She says –

'Why've you still got him with you?'

Right in front of him.

I've just had to pick him up

Stop the fighting

Tell him off

Clean his cuts

Wipe his tears.

Explain to him what

Gay means

Then explain to him the difference between

Gay men

Lesbian women.

See him realise his mum doesn't care about him

See him see a man not worthy of his mum

Of women

Maybe.

Then his nana

My mam

She says that

Now

In front of him.

I felt like answering her

Telling her

Straight

I've got to meet this court welfare officer, stop Joanne getting David back. I'm going to be there all afternoon. I would have took him to Angela's but you beat the sense out of her before she was old enough to realise. Made her vulnerable. Gullible to any fucking prick. A proper fallen angel. Only she didn't fall. You pulled her down. Dragged her by her hair. Kicking. Screaming. Pulling. Punching. So I can't leave him there. In the filth. The misery. In the failures of a women you never let be. I just can't. Not today. Not anymore. Not whilst this is going on. So unfortunately. So. Very. Fucking. Unfortunately. I've brought him here. To his nana's. His only nana's. Who still can't stand the, the skin he sings in. The skin he sulks in. The skin he sleeps. His skin. Can't see beyond fucking skin!

...

But I don't.

Then that look

That tainting look of fear

It's changed

It's

Satisfied

It's now a

I told you look

A

I told you so look

A

You should have had one of your own

Look.

Then

After that

I've

Won

Look

...

She lets us in

Into

DAVE *gets into the car.*

The music increases in volume – it twists and spikes.

The music battles itself – Rod Stewart – UB40 – Michael Jackson.

It gets louder and louder – the songs fight each other.

Eventually DAVE *stops the music.*

He rips the front seats out.

He brings them downstage one by one.

He turns them so they face each other.

He sits in one.

1992.

DAVE

'She left

She left him with me

There was never any problem with that,

> *'So...how long have you been the sole carer of the child?'*

'Nearly two years now'

> *'So...have you tried to help the child remain in contact with his mother?'*

'No

She left

Hasn't been back'

> '*So... You're saying the child's mother hasn't attempted to make any contact with her –*

'– I'm saying

I've been busy trying to raise my son'

UB40 plays quietly from the car stereo.

DAVE *notices.*

> '*So... How are you keeping the child engaged with his roots?*

'His roots?

What roots?

I'm his –'

> '*– So...you know? ...Food, clothes, culture, etcetera?*'

'He's from Manchester

He lives in Manchester

He's got culture'

> '*So... Being a white male*
>
> *How would you be able to provide for or respond to a child of colour's needs?*'

'You what?

Joanne's white'

> '*So... The mother also worked in a Afro-Caribbean hairdresser for a –*'

'– Oh fuck off!'

Just because she fucked a

A

Black man

Fucking

Nine years ago

Doesn't mean she knows anything more than me

About my son!'

DAVE *gets up and switches the music off.*

> '*So* –'

'– So no!

Nothing

Fuck it!'

> '*So…*'

DAVE *reluctantly sits back in the chair.*

> '*So…*'

'So?'

> '*So… There is a sense. A feeling. That the child chose to stay with you for reasons that may not be helpful to his development*'

'What?'

> '*So… There is another feeling that the child chose to stay with you because you prefer not to discipline him*'

'Is that what she's said?'

> '*So… Do you disagree? Have you not "taken a backseat" when it comes to discipline or focus for the child?,*'

'No. No I don't shout at him

Or smack him

I

Left that to Joanne'

> '*So… Why is that? Why don't you think you can discipline the child?*'

'I

I didn't because

I'm'

       'So... Do you think it may be because
       "biologically" you're not really in a
       position to -,

'– He chose me because he loves me.

Because I have a bond with him

Because he feels safe. Looked after.

He wouldn't want to stay with me if

If he didn't feel that'

       'So...–'

'– So nothing.

If Joanne didn't have any of that with him

Tuff. It's not my fault'

       'So –'

'– Do you know she's

She's gay?'

       'So... We are not here to discuss –'

'– How's that gonna help my lad?

Ey?

What male role models is he going to have?

Never mind

Black this

Black that

Who's going to teach him how to be a man?

Ey?

Do you how many fights he gets into

Because of this

Because of her

Her bullshit!'

             'So... Mr –'

'– I'll pay for a lawyer

I'm not doing this

I'll see her in court

Fuck this fucking bollocks'

DAVE *leans into the car and turns the music on.*

Irish music plays – from the juke box.

He grabs a beer from inside the car – opens it.

He sits on the bonnet.

DAVE *is in the pub – The Hanging Chandelier.*

Me – Cig – Mouth – Lighter – Flick – Spark – Flame – Smoke – ***INHALE.***

E

X

H

A

L

E

Hand – Glass – Mouth – Drink – Eyes – See – Paul – Pissed.

Pissed – Paul – Laughs – Points.

Fat bird – Pissed – Dances – Bad.

Paul – Pissed – Eyes – Perv – Possible – Fuck.

Me – Glass – Mouth – Drink – Glass – Table.

Hand – Cig – Drag – ***INHALE.***

Cig – Drag – ***INHALE.***

E

X

H

A

L

E

Paul – Pissed – Perving – Prick – Stands – Shouts – Sits –
Table – Knocked – Drinks – Spill – Both – Stand.

   'Shit'

'Yeah'

   'Sorry'

'Right'

   'Another?'

'Yeah'

   'Cigs?'

'Soaked'

   'Right'

Me – Chair – Sit – Paul – Bar – Stumbles – Towards.

Me – Cig – Ash – Flick – Cig – Drag – ***INHALE.***

E

X

H

A

L

E

Fat bird – Table – Stands – On.

Leg – Snap – Table – Break – Fat bird – Floor – Splat.

Paul – Laughter – Explodes – Top.

Over – He – Goes – Goes – Goes – Goes – Goes.

My – Head – Aches.

Cig – Drag – *INHALE.*

Cig – Drag – *INHALE.*

E

X

H

A

L

E

Paul – Returns – Drinks – Down.

Me – Glass – Mouth – Drink – Glass – Table.

Paul – Up – Fat bird – Talks – Laughs – Arse – Touch.

Me – Glass – Mouth – Drink – Glass – Table.

Cig – Drag – *INHALE.*

E

X

H

A

L

E

Paul – Fat bird – Talks – Laughs – Arse – Squeeze – Bloke – Sees.

Me – Glass – Mouth – Drink – Drink – Drink.

Cig – Drag – *INHALE.*

Cig – Drag – *INHALE.*

E

X

H

A

L

E

Bloke – Angry – Fat bird – Pull – Away – Paul – Fat bird – Pull – Towards.

Me – Cig – Ash – Tray – Kill – Cig.

Glass – Mouth – Drink – Finish.

Bloke – Paul – Heads – Butt.

Me – Glass – Hand – Stand – Walk – Towards – Bloke – Me – Hand – Bloke – Neck – Squeeze – Talk – Low –

'If you want to be wearing this fucking pint glass mate just carry on.

Well?

Right.

Fucking...'

Paul – Laughs – Agrees – Taunts – Bloke.

'Stop being a fucking arsehole Paul. Get a cloth, wipe that table. Prick'

> *'Right. Yeah. Sorry Dave. I just...a laugh. In it? Sorry. Right.'*

Me – Turn – Away – Toilet – Head – Towards – Door – Open – Toilet – In.

Hand – Glass – Wall – Smash.

Cubicle – Locked – Cubicle – Door – Kick – Cubicle – Door – Kick – Door – Kick.

Voice – Cubicle – Shouts –

> *'Alright mate give us a sec'*

'Stop doing drugs you fucking druggy cunt'

Condom machine – Punch – Hard – Punch – Again – Condom machine – Wall – Rip – Off.

Hands – Throb – Knuckles – Bleed – ***INHALE.***

E

X

H

A

L

E.

INHALE.

E

X

H

A

L

E

Toilet – Flush – Cubicle – Door – Open – Fella – Out – Sees – Blood – Sees – Wall – Sees – Me – *INHALE.*

E

X

H

A

L

E

Fella – Toilet – Out – Fast.

Me – Breath – Caught.

Hands – Sink – Wash

INHALE.

E

X

H

A

L

E

Mirror – Check – Belt – Shirt – Tuck – Belt – Adjust – *INHALE.*

Toilet – Out – Pub – Into – *EXHALE*

'Joanne'

INHALE.

See – Paul – See – Me – See – Joanne.

Paul – Pervs – Possible – Punch up.

Cunt.

Fucking cunt.

Table – Walk – Sit – Joanne – Avoid – Contact – Eyes – All – Everyone.

> *'At least she's not here with her fucking girlfriend.*
>
> *That'd be rubbing the salt in that Dave.*
>
> *Taking the piss just coming in here. In't she?*
>
> *In't she Dave? Cheeky slag'*

Me – Hands – Paul's – Head – Grab – Table – Paul's – Fucking face –

Slam – Slam – Slam

'Call her that again I'll fucking kill you'

INHALE – EXHALE – INHALE – EXHALE

Paul – Nose – Broke – Blood – Beer.

INHALE – EXHALE

> *'Sorry Dave. I'm sorry I...'*

Me – Pub – Everyone – Looks.

INHALE – EXHALE

Joanne – Sees.

INHALE

Me – Door – Exit – Fast

Out

Into

DAVE *puts the back seat on top of the car.*

He climbs up and sits on it.

He watches the pub.

E

X

H

A

L

E.

Then

Just as I'm thinking

Go home

Pick David up from Angela's

He's been there too long

Make him some teacakes

Let him watch *The Bill.*

The pub doors burst open

Paul's head being used to do the bursting

He falls forward onto the pavement

Scraping his chin

Scratching his knees

All sorts of drunken

Fucks

Slags

Slappers

Queers

Dykes

Escape from his mouth.

Then Joanne's at the doors with her

Her

You know.

Paul jumps up

Before I can see how

He's done it.

He's

Head-butted her.

He's broken her nose.

Joanne.

Then I

I

I fucking

DAVE *explodes.*

Dive head first

Into

Into

All the things I had left

In the past.

My youth

Wrong turns

Missteps

Regrets

Get backs.

Retracing my tracks

Trying to find something to

Anything to

Fuck.

I must get

Into

He destroys what's remaining of the car.

Into

'Look at me wrong mate

Yes you mate

You look at me like that again

You heard you

You fucking'

Fucking this

Fucking that

Running on empty

Driving on flats.

No car

But still

Burning rubber

Sucking the udder of the fat fucking cow.

Laughing at me

Fucking bitch

Into

He's violent – lost – fuming.

Into

Which drink

Which pub

'Which fucking cunt said that?

Who?

You?

Right'

Fight

Blood

Fight

Into

Another night

Night out

One of many

Bouncer

Punch.

Two bouncers

Fucking

Fat fight.

Blue lights

Punch

Copper

Blood.

Four pigs

Fight

Into

Back of the van

Pig van.

Fight

Bars

Knuckles

Punch

Door

Blood.

Police

Fight

Into

Station.

Desk sergeant

Fight

'Cunt'

Police

Hold

Grab

Force

Fucking

Frog-marched

By pigs

Into

Cell.

Wall

Fight

Hand

Blood

On blood.

Shout.

Scream.

Sit.

Sleep

Into

The car stereo remains.

DAVE *turns it on – though not connected to the car it still works.*

*"KIDS IN AMERICA"******** – by Kim Wilde Plays*

Into

Out.

Of the cell

Station

Sty.

Always

In

Out

Shake it all about.

Into

DAVE *scrambles through the scrap.*

Into

Which pub

Which drink

Which bird

Won't fuck

'Fuck off'

Bloke

'Right'

Blood

'Come on then!'

DAVE *turns on anything that can be turned on.*

Indicators – windscreen wipers – engines – etc.

******** A licence to produce SPARKPLUG does not include a performance licence for "KIDS IN AMERICA". For further information, please see Music Use Note on page v.

This goes on for some time – DAVE is lost in everything that he shouldn't be.

The sounds morph – just like DAVE's soberness – painful and dangerous.

Everything builds to an almost unbearable state until.

DAVE *lets out one long bellow!*

He holds his leg.

Everything stops.

...

I remember getting my first car. Just after you... Once you'd... after you died. I was determined to get a car. Get a job. Be a man. Look after...everyone. The family.

I fell out of love with football straight into pissing about. Driving around Wythenshawe. Car full of mates. Looking for birds. For a laugh. For a scrap with anyone who wasn't from round here. Round our way.

It was my way or the fucking long road mate.

This was our song. Don't know why it was just... It... It was freedom. The car. The music.

Loud. Louder

DAVE *turns the music up. Kim Wilde–* **"KIDS IN AMERICA"**********.

He sticks his head out of a window – sings along.

We owned it. I owned it. The car. The pub. The street. The rep. The record. Constantly fighting. Constantly in the nick.

******** A licence to produce SPARKPLUG does not include a performance licence for "KIDS IN AMERICA". For further information, please see Music Use Note on page v.

Over nothing. Just...me. Letting off steam. Taking it out on one too many innocents.

The music lowers and slows down.

I was in Strangeways, looking at fifteen months. I was nineteen. I'd been in a week when Angela's fella at the time. What was his name? Can't remember but he paid my bail. Just paid it. About four hundred quid. In one go. No mither. Romance that. Rescuing your bird's big brother from jail to try stop her crying at night. Proper he was. Was he Craig's Dad? Fucking hell, can't remember now. Bad that.

I remember getting out of his car thinking, this is it. This is my fresh start. Stop pissing about. Be a man. Be good. Be OK with...with you. Not being...here.

Then just as I was being what I needed to be. Figuring it all out. Calming down. That fucking car. Gone before I knew it was there. But it was there. Was there long enough to send me up, over it, fifteen feet in the air.

Landed on the curb you know?

Exactly half of me.

Shattered.

Mam says I've got your limp now

The music dies.

Died twice the nurses said.

Never play football again

The doctor said.

The police said

The car drove away

I was left for dead.

...

I reckon one of my victims drove that car.

...

No more fighting

I said.

Then

Got out

Out of hospital

Out of the wheelchair

Into the

The Capri

Into

Joanne

Into

DAVE *sits with the cassette player.*

He presses play – it doesn't work.

Into

DAVE *pulls himself together.*

Dusts himself off.

He clears a path through the parts of cars on the stage.

He stands at the far end of the path – furthest from us.

Into

1993.

DAVE

Twenty steps.

Feels

Strange.

I feel

I don't know.

I don't know

It frightens me.

Nineteen steps.

Yeah.

I feel scared.

I'm scared.

Empty.

Nothing.

I know I can't be that.

I can't do nothing

You never let me.

Be someone

Make sure you do something.

Eighteen.

Seventeen steps.

Shit.

He's gonna see me soon.

He'll see me

He'll think I'm back.

I'm not sure if I am

Back.

Back.

Eighteen steps.

I'm back from my missing week.

Me pissed

Seeking

Something

Someone to

Fight mainly.

Fighting my way back to Joanne but

Well

Yeah

That ship has sailed.

Truly.

My car is scrapped

I'm now

Seventeen.

Sixteen.

Fifteen steps

From David getting me back.

From being David's something.

Fifteen steps

From running away to my own.

Nothing.

Empty.

Plenty of others

Could

Would.

Leave him.

I can't.

Even though my own mam insists that I should

Again.

Leave

So I can live

Raise my own.

I can't.

He is.

No choice.

I don't think.

I've too much of you in me.

Fourteen.

Thirteen.

Twelve steps

He'll be able to make out it's me.

His fat little face will light up

He'll see

His best mate.

Me.

Limping towards him.

Not picking him up in the Sierra

Not anymore.

No car.

No more.

Eleven.

Ten steps

Then I'll have David.

That's all I'll need.

Want.

Ever.

Nine steps.

I hope.

Eight steps

Cars can take a back seat.

A to B will be done by feet.

Seven more steps

Then I'm going to lift him up on my shoulder.

One last time.

Before he gets older

Before he remembers these weeks.

The weeks where I went missing.

Trying to find something

But only finding sweaty beds

With wrap around legs.

Beer.

No patience

Police stations.

Six.

Five more steps

Then I can't make this mistake again.

Four more steps

I'm no longer his best friend.

Three more steps

I'll be a lot more than that.

Two more steps

I'll be

His Dad.

One more step.

His everything.

David's.

Forever.

No more steps

No turning back.

No more steps

I'll be someone

Something to someone.

No more steps

I'm closer to you.

No more steps

I'm further from what she wants for me.

No more steps

No more car.

No more lifts.

No more for all

Everywhere.

No more steps

Wherever David's going I'll take him.

Me.

No more steps

I hope

I hope I'll be

I'll be as good a Man

As good a Dad

As good a

Dave

As you.

DAVE *leaves the stage.*

The stage is almost bare.

...

DAVID *(10) runs in – plays with the car parts that remain.*

In between the selection and placement of car parts he says –.

                    'AND...

AND...

AND...'

DAVID

And I've just been swimming with Aunty Angela.

And it was top.

And I get out of her blue beetle-bug car

And straight onto Uncle Paul's bike.

And Uncle Paul's top.

And he lets me sit on the handle bars.

And Uncle Paul becomes a snake monster.

And I fall off.

And it hurts a bit.

And Paul's laughing.

And so I don't cry.

And I ask if I can get on the back this time

And Paul says no

And so I sit back on the handle bars.

And Uncle Paul asks me loads of questions about swimming.

And racing.

And the man who asked me for a race in the swimming pool.

And I tell Paul the man was my Mum's friend

And Paul pulls the brakes.

And I fall off again.

And Paul doesn't laugh.

And I cry.

And Paul tells me to shut up.

And now we're walking

And Paul's talking about this big black man who asked me for a race.

And I tell him it was my Mum's friend

And Paul stops.

And he tells me to listen to him.

And he asks me what the man's name was.

And I say I can't remember.

And Paul asks me if he looked like anyone I know

And I say no.

And Paul says that his name was Ainsley

And Paul says he's your real Dad.

And he sort of pulls my hair.

And then he says something else.

And then he says afro.

And I say what do you mean Paul?

And he says why do you think you've got big lips and fat feet?

And he says again that Dave's not my real Dad.

And he says my Mum lied to me.

And I really don't know what he's talking about.

And I don't say much for the rest of the way back.

And I think it doesn't matter I'll just ask Dad.

And I get home.

And Paul leaves.

And my Dad's top.

And he toasts me some teacakes

And he puts loads of butter on.

And he lets me stay up for *The Bill*.

Makes himself a bed on a back seat and gets into it.

> And he fixes my headphones with Sellotape so that I can listen to Michael Jackson on my Walkman.
>
> And he puts me to bed in his bed.
>
> And he kisses me goodnight.

*He presses play on the cassette player – Michael Jackson's "**BAD**"******** album plays – quietly.*

> And I say Dad?
>
> And he says what?
>
> And I say who's Ainsley?
>
> And my Dad says why?
>
> And I say this big black man my Mum's friend asked me for a race at swimming
>
> Not the length
>
> Just the width
>
> And I won.
>
> Twice.
>
> And he was massive
>
> And I won.
>
> And he said he knew my mum he was her friend.
>
> And Paul said Mum had lied
>
> And that he was my real Dad.
>
> Ainsley.
>
> Not you.
>
> And I told him to shut up.
>
> But what's he going on about Dad?

******** A licence to produce SPARKPLUG does not include a performance licence for the "BAD" album. For further information, please see Music Use Note on page v.

And Dad's face looks like it did when I first saw him cry.

That time when he promised that he would never get married again.

It's just us now forever he said then.

And now he says

He says

My Dad says Paul's right.

Ainsley is my Dad.

My real one.

My blood one.

And I said what?

And Dad said again that Ainsley is my real Dad

Your black one.

And I say what the hell are you talking about Dad?

And then Dad

Dad

My Dad

He says

My Dad says

David

You don't have to call me Dad

Anymore

If you don't want to.

You can just call me Dave

And I said

What?

Shut up

You big divvy!

Why the hell would I do that?

Bone head!

He puts the headphones of his Walkman on and settles for sleep.

As the batteries on David's Walkman die out – so do the lights and music.

The End

ALTERNATIVE PROLOGUE

Pre-Set

House-lights.

The stage is littered with tyres and batteries – exhausts and sparkplugs – spare parts of a Ford Escort – and Capri – the remains of a Fiat 126 – bits and bobs of various Vauxhalls and other spare parts belonging to other retro cars.

DAVID *(now) plays with the car parts as the audience enter.*

As the audience settle – the lights change.

Prologue

DAVID

I've got two dads

One's black

That makes me

Black

I suppose

So I'm told.

I've got two dads

One's black

One's white

I'm half-caste

They say

Others say

I'm coloured

Some say

Mixed race.

I've got two dads

I've never met the

Black one

Or his others

His family

My sisters

Brothers.

I've got two dads

The black

Keeps me distanced from

The white ones family

That really bothers me.

I've got two dads

One holds me up

Shows me to the world

Guides me through my

Mistakes

Stupidity

The only thing

The black one gave me was

Ethnicity

Sometimes I can hate that about me.

I've got two dads

One played with me for hours

Days

Years

The other

Left when I was

Minus eight months old.

I've got two dads

One of them is hardly a

Man

Was never really mine

The other was also

My Mum

For a time.

I've got two Dads

One is from Jamaica

My mother says

One of them is the

Greatest dad in the world

I says.

I've got two dads

One of them is my father

The other is just

A cock

With balls

...

And...

DAVID *finds his headphones and Walkman.*

And...

DAVID *finds his dummy and tickle (comfort blanket).*

And...

DAVID *makes himself a bed on a backseat.*

And...

He puts the headphones of his Walkman on.

And...

He settles for sleep.

He presses play –

Michael Jackson's **"BAD"** *album plays from the car radio.* **"SMOOTH CRIMINAL"** *plays – it rewinds – fast forwards –* **"MAN IN THE MIRROR"** *plays – it rewinds – fast forwards –* **"THE WAY YOU MAKE ME FEEL"** *plays – it rewinds – fast forwards –* **"I JUST CAN'T STOP LOVING YOU"** *plays – it rewinds – fast forwards –* **"BAD"** *plays – it slows down – like a Walkman on its last legs.**

As the batteries on David's Walkman die out – so do the lights and music.

Lights fade.

Lights up.

1993.

DAVE *(35) appears.*

He gets into the car

He searches in the glove box – finds a tape – inserts it into the cassette player.

He presses play

Rod Stewart's – **"TONIGHT'S THE NIGHT"** *plays.***

DAVE *sits in a car seat downstage – he holds the steering wheel/gearstick.*

---

* A licence to produce SPARKPLUG does not include a performance licence for "SMOOTH CRIMINAL", "MAN IN THE MIRROR", "THE WAY YOU MAKE ME FEEL", "I JUST CAN'T STOP LOVING YOU", "BAD" . For further information, please see Music Use Note on page v.
** A licence to produce SPARKPLUG does not include a performance licence for "TONIGHT'S THE NIGHT". For further information, please see Music Use Note on page v.

VISIT THE SAMUEL FRENCH BOOKSHOP AT THE ROYAL COURT THEATRE

Browse plays and theatre books, get expert advice and enjoy a coffee

Samuel French Bookshop
Royal Court Theatre
Sloane Square
London
SW1W 8AS
020 7565 5024

Shop from thousands of titles on our website

 samuelfrench.co.uk

 samuelfrenchltd

 samuel french uk

Lightning Source UK Ltd.
Milton Keynes UK
UKHW011245060219
336838UK00005B/384/P

9 780573 116216